Fun Guessing Games About 100 Famous Americans in History!

Sunflower
education
Exceptional Books for Teachers and Parents

Progressively more detailed clues slowly reveal an important figure from American history. Try it!

1. I am a man who lived from 1847 to 1931.
2. As a child, I loved to read science books and build models.
3. I founded 14 companies, including General Electric.
4. I was known as "the Wizard of Menlo Park."
5. I invented the light bulb!

How many clues until you guessed Thomas Edison?

Instructions show you how to turn these simple quizzes into powerful teaching tools. Use them as warm ups, wrap ups, and even assessments! Kids love to play so they make a perfect reward. You can play in large and small groups, on teams, with and without points, and even on the included game board. A proven winner with students!

Grades 4 and Up • 100 Historical Figures

Introduction explains many different ways to play.

Please feel free to photocopy the sheets in this book within reason. Sunflower Education grants teachers permission to photocopy the sheets from this book for educational use. This permission is granted to individual teachers and not entire schools or school systems. For information or questions regarding permissions, please send an email to permissions@SunflowerEducation.net.

Visit **SunflowerEducation.Net** for more great books!

Editorial   Sunflower Education
Design   Blue Agave Studio

ISBN-13: 978-1-937166-10-6
ISBN-10: 1-937166-10-4
Copyright © 2011
Sunflower Education
All rights reserved.
Printed in the U.S.A.

Contents

To the Teacher 1
Answer Key 7

1. Abigail Adams 9
2. John Adams 9
3. John Quincy Adams 10
4. Susan B. Anthony 10
5. Neil Armstrong 11
6. Clara Barton 11
7. Alexander Graham Bell 12
8. William Bradford 12
9. John Brown 13
10. William Jennings Bryan 13
11. John C. Calhoun 14
12. Andrew Carnegie 14
13. Cesar Chavez 15
14. Henry Clay 15
15. Bill Clinton 16
16. Calvin Coolidge 16
17. James Fenimore Cooper 17
18. Francisco Vasquez de Coronado 17
19. Charles Coughlin 18
20. George A. Custer 18
21. Jefferson Davis 19
22. Jack Dempsey 19
23. Dorothea Dix 20
24. Frederick Douglass 20
25. W.E.B. Du Bois 21
26. Amelia Earhart 21
27. Thomas Edison 22
28. Albert Einstein 22
29. Dwight D. Eisenhower 23
30. Ralph Waldo Emerson 23
31. Enrico Fermi 24
32. F. Scott Fitzgerald 24
33. Stephen Foster 25
34. Benjamin Franklin 25
35. Betty Friedan 26
36. William Lloyd Garrison 26
37. Ulysses S. Grant 27
38. Alexander Hamilton 27
39. Ernest Hemingway 28
40. Herbert Hoover 28
41. Andrew Jackson 29
42. Thomas Jefferson 29
43. John Paul Jones 30
44. Helen Keller 30
45. Florence Kelley 31
46. John F. Kennedy 31
47. Martin Luther King, Jr. 32
48. Robert E. Lee 32
49. Meriwether Lewis 33
50. Sinclair Lewis 33

51. Abraham Lincoln	34
52. Charles Lindbergh	34
53. Benjamin Lundy	35
54. James Madison	35
55. Horace Mann	36
56. John Marshall	36
57. Thurgood Marshall	37
58. Cyrus McCormick	37
59. James Monroe	38
60. J. P. Morgan	38
61. Samuel F. B. Morse	39
62. Annie Oakley	39
63. Barack Obama	40
64. Sandra Day O'Connor	40
65. Thomas Paine	41
66. Rosa Parks	41
67. Frances Perkins	42
68. Ronald Reagan	42
69. Sally Ride	43
70. Jackie Robinson	43
71. John D. Rockefeller	44
72. Eleanor Roosevelt	44
73. Franklin D. Roosevelt	45
74. Sacagawea	45
75. Dred Scott	46
76. Upton Sinclair	46
77. Sitting Bull (Tatanka Yotanka)	47
78. John Smith	47
79. Squanto	48
80. Elizabeth Cady Stanton	48
81. Harriet Beecher Stowe	49
82. William Graham Sumner	49
83. William Howard Taft	50
84. Ida Tarbell	50
85. Zachary Taylor	51
86. Henry David Thoreau	51
87. Bill Tilden	52
88. Harry S. Truman	52
89. Frederick Jackson Turner	53
90. Mark Twain	53
91. Cornelius Vanderbilt	54
92. Amerigo Vespucci	54
93. George Washington	55
94. Booker T. Washington	55
95. Eli Whitney	56
96. Walt Whitman	56
97. Orville Wright	57
98. Wilbur Wright	57
99. Woodrow Wilson	58
100. Brigham Young	58

To The Teacher

Welcome to *Who Am I? Fun Guessing Games About 100 Famous Americans in History!*

Who Am I? is both a simple teaching tool and a powerful classroom resource. It's simple because it works on a basic, easy-to-understand premise: gradually revealing more and better clues until a mystery is solved. It's powerful because this technique can be utilized in a variety of ways to reach and delight kids.

Why Students Love It

Everyone loves a good mystery, and that's a big part of **Who Am I?**'s appeal. Also, when kids are giving the clues, they enjoy the prestige of being "in the know"; when they are guessing, they enjoy the chance to demonstrate their knowledge—and win the game.

The Historical Figures

Who Am I? provides guessing games about 100 famous people in American history. A quick glance at the Table of Contents tells you who they are. These individuals were selected because they played notable roles in American history and are widely studied in school. Educated Americans are expected to be familiar with these people and their accomplishments. The list was also designed to portray people from a variety of endeavors. So the list includes political and military figures as well as inventors, authors, and astronauts. For ease of use, the figures are presented alphabetically by last name.

The Guessing Games

Five clues are provided for each historical figure. The clues are in the first person, as if spoken by the actual individual. The five clues are arranged in a sort of inverted pyramid, from the most general (Clue 1) to most specific (Clue 5).

Typically, the clues provide these types of information, with Clue 1 being consistent, Clues 2-4 in various orders, and Clue 5 close to a giveaway.

1. Gender and life dates
2. Geographical region
3. General skills or knowledge
4. Historical context
5. Specific accomplishment

How to Play

The basic game is simple. The person playing the historical figure asks aloud *"Who Am I?"* He or she then reads the first clue and asks "Do you know who I am?" If no one knows, the person playing the historical figure reads the next clue and asks "Do you know who I am?" The process is repeated until the historical figure is identified or not.

How to Use the Game as an Educational Tool

Teachers and homeschool parents have used *Who Am I?* in a variety of ways. In fact, the game's simplicity combined with its flexibility make it a powerful teaching tool.

- **As a Warm-up** Focusing students at the beginning of the day or instructional period is vital. A few rounds of *Who Am I?* can do the trick.
- **As Assessment** Like matching on a test, a *Who Am I?* quiz will reveal whether students know a historical figure from a description.
- **As a Close** A few games of *Who Am I?* offers students a chance to "cool down" after a long day but still functions as good instructional time.
- **As a Reward** Kids like playing this game: it's simple and fun. Teachers can organize teams and even tournament play.

Large Group Play Read the clues to the class. Students raise their hands or shout out answers when they solve the riddle. As an alternative, you designate students to read the clues aloud to the class. Two or three students at the head of the classroom taking turns works well.

Small Group Play Organize the class into several groups. Within each group, a designated student gives the clues, or the group members take turns.

Team Play Organize the class into two or more teams. The teams compete against each other for a set amount of time or points (see "Playing with Points").

"Baseball" A variation of team play. Designate locations in your classroom to serve as first base, second base, third base, and home, to create a mock baseball diamond. Organize the class into two teams. To begin play, a player from one team walks to home. You present the clue. If the player fails to identify the historical figure, he or she is out. The next player at bat is given one additional clue. Three outs and the side is out, and the other team is at bat. If he or she correctly identifies the person, bases are awarded according to the following:

Who Am I? Baseball	
Number of Clues Given Before Correct Answer	Bases Awarded
1	Home run
2	Home run
3	Triple
4	Double
5	Single

Players advance physically around the bases. The game is over at the end of a set number of innings.

Partner Play Pairs of students can take turns giving clues to each other.

Playing With Points Point play is also possible. You can award students greater numbers of points based on the fewer number of clues (see the table).

Who Am I? Point System	
Number of Clues Given Before Correct Answer	Points Awarded/Squares Advanced
1	5
2	4
3	3
4	2
5	1

Playing With the Game Board The game board can be copied and used to play *Who Am I?* as a traditional board game. You can also copy and cut out the figures to use as tokens. Using the board, players advance one square for each time they are first to identify the individual. Point play is also possible; multiple squares are advanced according to when the historical figure is identified (see the table). The playing board is on the following page. Two "Finish" boxes are provided for long and short games.

Card Play You can cut each quiz out and use the quizzes as cards. Cards can be distributed to students in a variety of ways. Students can pick cards at random as a station exercise.

Grouping See the table for suggested grouping of quizzes or cards.

Have Fun!

Whatever form *Who Am I?* takes in your classroom or homeschool environment, we hope you and your students have a great time. Learning, after all, should be fun! If you get a chance, drop us a line at info@sunflowereducation.net and tell us about it!

Start ⬇

1	2	3	4	5 ⬇
10 ⬇	9	8	7	6
11	12	13	14	15 ⬇
20 ⬇	19	18	17	16 Finish
21	22	23	24	25 ⬇
30 ⬇	29	28	27	26
31	32	33	34	34 ⬇

Finish

4 Who Am I? SunflowerEducation.net

Game Tokens

Copy this page and cut out the shapes to use as game tokens on the game board. The game board is on page 4.

Suggested Groupings

Abolitionists	9. John Brown; 36. William Lloyd Garrison; 53. Benjamin Lundy; 81. Harriet Beecher Stowe
Authors	17. James Fenimore Cooper; 30. Ralph Waldo Emerson; 32. F. Scott Fitzgerald; 39. Ernest Hemingway; 44. Helen Keller; 50. Sinclair Lewis; 65. Thomas Paine; 76. Upton Sinclair; 81. Harriet Beecher Stowe; 82. William Graham Sumner; 86. Henry David Thoreau; 89. Frederick Jackson Turner; 90. Mark Twain; 94. Booker T. Washington; 96. Walt Whitman; 84. Ida Tarbell
Aviators	26. Amelia Earhart; 52. Charles Lindbergh; 97. Orville Wright; 98. Wilbur Wright
Businessmen	12. Andrew Carnegie; 60. J.P. Morgan; 71. John D. Rockefeller; 91. Cornelius Vanderbilt
Celebrities	22. Jack Dempsey; 62. Annie Oakley; 70. Jackie Robinson; 87. Bill Tilden; 33. Stephen Foster
Civil Rights Leaders	4. Susan B. Anthony; 13. Cesar Chavez; 23. Dorothea Dix; 24. Frederick Douglass; 25. W.E.B. Du Bois; 35. Betty Friedan; 45. Florence Kelley; 47. Martin Luther King, Jr.; 67. Frances Perkins; 72. Eleanor Roosevelt; 80. Elizabeth Cady Stanton
Religious Figures	19. Charles Coughlin; 100. Brigham Young
Explorers	5. Neil Armstrong; 18. Francisco Vasquez de Coronado; 49. Meriwether Lewis; 69. Sally Ride; 92. Amerigo Vespucci
Military Leaders	20. George A. Custer; 37. Ulysses S. Grant; 43. John Paul Jones; 48. Robert E. Lee; 77. Sitting Bull (Tatanka Yotanka); 85. Zachary Taylor; 93. George Washington
Famous Native Americans	74. Sacagawea; 77. Sitting Bull (Tatanka Yotanka); 79. Squanto
Founding Fathers	2. John Adams; 34. Benjamin Franklin; 93. George Washington
Great Women	1. Abigail Adams; 4. Susan B. Anthony; 6. Clara Barton; 23. Dorothea Dix; 26. Amelia Earhart; 35. Betty Friedan; 44. Helen Keller; 45. Florence Kelley; 62. Annie Oakley; 64. Sandra Day O'Connor; 66. Rosa Parks; 67. Frances Perkins; 69. Sally Ride; 72. Eleanor Roosevelt; 74. Sacagawea; 80. Elizabeth Cady Stanton; 81. Harriet Beecher Stowe; 84. Ida Tarbell
Inventors	7. Alexander Graham Bell; 27. Thomas Edison; 58. Cyrus McCormick; 61. Samuel F. B. Morse; 95. Eli Whitney
Leaders	8. William Bradford; 10. William Jennings Bryan; 14. Henry Clay; 38. Alexander Hamilton; 55. Horace Mann; 11. John C. Calhoun
Leaders of American Groups	21. Jefferson Davis; 77. Sitting Bull (Tatanka Yotanka); 78. John Smith; 100. Brigham Young
Presidents	2. John Adams; 3. John Quincy Adams; 15. Bill Clinton; 16. Calvin Coolidge; 29. Dwight D. Eisenhower; 37. Ulysses S. Grant; 40. Herbert Hoover; 41. Andrew Jackson; 42. Thomas Jefferson; 46. John F. Kennedy; 51. Abraham Lincoln; 54. James Madison; 59. James Monroe; 63. Barack Obama; 68. Ronald Reagan; 73. Franklin D. Roosevelt; 83. William Howard Taft; 85. Zachary Taylor; 88. Harry S. Truman; 93. George Washington; 99. Woodrow Wilson
Scientists	28. Albert Einstein; 31. Enrico Fermi
Supreme Court Justices	56. John Marshall; 57. Thurgood Marshall; 64. Sandra Day O'Connor

Answer Key

1. Abigail Adams
2. John Adams
3. John Quincy Adams
4. Susan B. Anthony
5. Neil A. Armstrong
6. Clara Barton
7. Alexander Graham Bell
8. William Bradford
9. John Brown
10. William Jennings Bryan
11. John C. Calhoun
12. Andrew Carnegie
13. Cesar Chavez
14. Henry Clay
15. Bill Clinton
16. Calvin Coolidge
17. James Fenimore Cooper
18. Francisco Vasquez de Coronado
19. Charles Coughlin
20. George A. Custer
21. Jefferson Davis
22. Jack Dempsey
23. Dorothea Dix
24. Frederick Douglass
25. W.E.B. Du Bois
26. Amelia Earhart
27. Thomas Edison
28. Albert Einstein
29. Dwight D. Eisenhower
30. Ralph Waldo Emerson
31. Enrico Fermi
32. F. Scott Fitzgerald
33. Stephen Foster
34. Benjamin Franklin
35. Betty Friedan
36. William Lloyd Garrison
37. Ulysses S. Grant
38. Alexander Hamilton
39. Ernest Hemingway
40. Herbert Hoover
41. Andrew Jackson
42. Thomas Jefferson
43. John Paul Jones
44. Helen Keller
45. Florence Kelley
46. John F. Kennedy
47. Martin Luther King
48. Robert E. Lee
49. Meriwether Lewis
50. Sinclair Lewis
51. Abraham Lincoln
52. Charles Lindbergh
53. Benjamin Lundy
54. James Madison
55. Horace Mann
56. John Marshall
57. Thurgood Marshall
58. Cyrus McCormick
59. James Monroe
60. J. P. Morgan
61. Samuel F. B. Morse
62. Annie Oakley
63. Barack Obama
64. Sandra Day O'Connor
65. Thomas Paine
66. Rosa Parks
67. Frances Perkins
68. Ronald Reagan
69. Sally Ride
70. Jackie Robinson
71. John D. Rockefeller
72. Eleanor Roosevelt
73. Franklin D. Roosevelt
74. Sacagawea
75. Dred Scott
76. Upton Sinclair
77. Sitting Bull (Tatanka Yotanka)
78. John Smith
79. Squanto
80. Elizabeth Cady Stanton
81. Harriet Beecher Stowe
82. William Graham Sumner
83. William Howard Taft
84. Ida Tarbell
85. Zachary Taylor
86. Henry David Thoreau
87. Bill Tilden
88. Harry S. Truman
89. Frederick Jackson Turner
90. Mark Twain
91. Cornelius Vanderbilt
92. Amerigo Vespucci
93. Booker T. Washington
94. George Washington
95. Walt Whitman
96. Eli Whitney
97. Woodrow Wilson
98. Orville Wright
99. Wilbur Wright
100. Brigham Young

1

❶ I am a woman who lived from 1744 to 1818.

❷ I was one of the few women of my time to be familiar with philosophy, political science, and literature.

❸ The letters I wrote have helped people understand what my times were really like.

❹ I was the mother of the sixth president of the United States.

❺ I was the second First Lady of the United States.

 Who Am I? _____

2

❶ I am a man who lived from 1735 to 1826.

❷ I was a vocal opponent of the Stamp Act.

❸ I nominated George Washington to be commander-in-chief of the Continental Army.

❹ I was the first vice president of the United States.

❺ I was the second president of the United States.

 Who Am I? _____

3

1. I am a man who lived from 1767 to 1848.
2. I was Secretary of State to James Monroe.
3. I was the sixth President of the United States.
4. John and Abigail Adams were my parents.
5. I was the first son of a President to become President.

Who Am I? _____

4

1. I am a woman who lived from 1820 to 1906.
2. I learned to read and write at age 3.
3. I gave 75 to 100 speeches a year for most of my life.
4. I appear on a coin.
5. I spent my life working for women's suffrage.

Who Am I? _____

5

❶ I am a man who was born in 1930.

❷ I was a Boy Scout.

❸ I flew test planes for the Air Force.

❹ I was an astronaut.

❺ I was the first person to set foot on the moon!

 Who Am I? _____

6

❶ I am a woman who lived from 1821 to 1912.

❷ When I was 11, I nursed my brother for three years after an injury.

❸ I was a nurse for soldiers during the Civil War.

❹ I was known as the "Angel of the Battlefield."

❺ I organized the American branch of the Red Cross.

 Who Am I? _____

7

1. I am a man who lived from 1847 to 1922.
2. Both my mother and my wife were deaf.
3. I invented hearing aids and studied sound.
4. My assistant's name was Watson.
5. I created the Bell Telephone Company.

 _____

8

1. I am a man who lived from 1590 to 1657.
2. I was a Puritan.
3. I signed the Mayflower Compact.
4. I wrote *Of Plimoth Plantation*.
5. I was elected 30 times to be Governor of Plymouth.

 _____

9

1. I am a man who lived from 1800 to 1859.
2. I was an abolitionist.
3. I led the Pottawatomie Massacre, where seven slave owners were killed.
4. I was executed by a hangman.
5. I led the raid on Harper's Ferry in 1859.

 Who Am I? _____

10

1. I am a man who lived from 1860 to 1925.
2. My nickname was "the Great Commoner."
3. As a politician, I opposed the gold standard, railroads, and large companies.
4. I gave a speech known as "The Cross of Gold."
5. I represented the World Christian Fundamentals Association in the Scopes Trial.

 Who Am I? _____

11

1. I am a man who lived from 1782 to 1850.
2. I was a "War Hawk."
3. I supported adding Texas to the union as a slave state.
4. I was Vice President under Andrew Jackson and John Quincy Adams.
5. Although I died before the Civil War, my thoughts about nullification, slavery and states' rights helped inspire my fellow Southerners to secede.

 Who Am I? _____

12

1. I am a man who lived from 1835 to 1919.
2. I worked in a factory when I was 13.
3. I was known as a "Captain of Industry."
4. I owned the largest steel company in the world.
5. I established hundreds of public libraries, as well as a famous concert hall in New York City.

 Who Am I? _____

Who Am I?

13

1. I am a man who lived from 1927 to 1993.
2. I was self-taught; I didn't even finish the eighth grade.
3. When I was young, I worked on farms.
4. I spoke Spanish and English.
5. I founded the United Farm Workers to support the rights of Hispanic workers.

 Who Am I? _____

14

1. I am a man who lived from 1777 to 1852.
2. I was called a "War Hawk" and urged the country to war with England in the War of 1812.
3. I represented Kentucky in both the Senate and the House of Representatives.
4. I helped create the Compromise of 1850, which concerned whether new states would be free or slave.
5. I am known as the "Great Compromiser."

 Who Am I? _____

Who Am I?

15

1. I am a man who was born in 1946.
2. I was born in Hope, Arkansas.
3. I was governor of Arkansas.
4. My wife's name is Hillary.
5. I was the 42nd President of the United States.

 Who Am I? _____

16

1. I am a man who lived from 1872 to 1933.
2. I was born on the Fourth of July.
3. I was famous for being very spare with my words.
4. I was president during the Roaring Twenties.
5. They called me "Silent Cal."

 Who Am I? _____

17

1. I am a man who lived from 1789 to 1851.
2. I enrolled at Yale when I was 13, but was expelled for childish pranks.
3. My father was a Congressman.
4. I was a writer.
5. I wrote *The Last of the Mohicans*.

 Who Am I? _____

18

1. I am a man who lived from 1510(?) to 1554.
2. I was born in Salamanca, Spain.
3. I was a conquistador.
4. I explored present-day northern Mexico and the American Southwest.
5. I was looking for the Seven Cities of Cibola.

 Who Am I? _____

19

1. I am a man who lived from 1891 to 1979.
2. I was born in Ontario, Canada.
3. I was a Catholic priest.
4. I spoke out against Roosevelt, World War II, the monetary system, and many other things.
5. I was one of the first people to use the radio to reach a very large audience.

Who Am I? _____

20

1. I am a man who lived from 1839 to 1876.
2. I graduated from West Point.
3. During the Civil War, I fought for the Union.
4. I was known as "the Boy General."
5. I led the U.S. Army forces in the Battle of Little Bighorn.

Who Am I? _____

Who Am I?

21

1. I am a man who lived from 1808 to 1889.
2. I fought in the Mexican-American War.
3. I was a slave owner.
4. I was a Senator from Mississippi before the Civil War.
5. I was the President of the Confederate States of America.

Who Am I? _____

22

1. I am a man who lived from 1895 to 1983.
2. I was of Irish and Cherokee descent.
3. My nickname was the "Manassa Mauler."
4. I was one of the greatest boxers of all time.
5. I fought Gene Tunney in 1926 and 1927.

Who Am I? _____

23

1. I am a woman who lived from 1802 to 1887.
2. I ran away from home at age 12.
3. During the Civil War, I served as Superintendent of the Army Nurses.
4. I lead the drive to build hospitals for the mentally ill.
5. My initials were D.D.!

Who Am I? _____

24

1. I am a man who lived from 1817 to 1895.
2. I was born a slave.
3. I learned to read even though it was against the law.
4. I wrote my autobiography in order to demonstrate the evils of slavery.
5. I was a great orator.

Who Am I? _____

25

❶ I am a man who lived from 1868 to 1963.

❷ I was the President of the National Association for the Advancement of Colored People (NAACP) for many years.

❸ I was the first African American graduate of Harvard University.

❹ I predicted that the chief problem of the 20th century would be "the color line."

❺ I wrote *The Souls of Black Folk*.

Who Am I? _____

26

❶ I am a woman who lived from 1897 to 1937(?).

❷ When I was 7, I built a small rollercoaster in my backyard.

❸ I was the first woman to fly across the Atlantic Ocean.

❹ I began a flight around the world in 1937.

❺ I disappeared on a solo flight over the Pacific Ocean.

Who Am I? _____

27

1. I am a man who lived from 1847 to 1931.
2. As a child, I loved to read science books and build models.
3. I founded 14 companies, including General Electric.
4. I was known as "the Wizard of Menlo Park."
5. I invented the light bulb!

 Who Am I? _____

28

1. I am a man who lived from 1879 to 1955.
2. I didn't speak until I was three years old, and some people thought I was slow.
3. I came to America in 1933 to escape Nazi Germany.
4. My name is synonymous with "genius."
5. I developed the theory of relativity.

 Who Am I? _____

29

1. I am a man who lived from 1890 to 1969.
2. My wife's name was Mamie.
3. I was the supreme commander of the Allied Forces in Europe during World War II.
4. I was also the supreme commander of NATO forces after the war.
5. I was the 34th president of the United States.

Who Am I? _____

30

1. I am a man who lived from 1803 to 1882.
2. I was ordained as a pastor.
3. Henry David Thoreau was one of my friends.
4. I was a Transcendentalist.
5. I wrote "Self-Reliance" as well as many other essays and poems.

Who Am I? _____

31

1. I am a man who lived from 1901 to 1954.
2. I was born in Italy but moved to America when I was 37.
3. I designed the first nuclear reactor.
4. I won the Nobel Prize in Physics in 1938.
5. I worked on the Manhattan Project, which created the first atomic bomb.

Who Am I? _____

32

1. I am a man who lived from 1896 to 1940.
2. My wife's name was Zelda.
3. I coined the term "Jazz Age."
4. I was a member of the "Lost Generation."
5. I wrote *The Great Gatsby*.

Who Am I? _____

33

1. I am a man who lived from 1826 to 1864.
2. I wrote my first song when I was 14.
3. I am known as the "Father of American Music."
4. I wrote "Beautiful Dreamer."
5. I also wrote "Oh! Susanna," "Camptown Races," and "Old Folks at Home" (also known as "Way Down Upon the Swanee River").

Who Am I? _____

34

1. I am a man who lived from 1706 to 1790.
2. I was a printer's apprentice.
3. I invented bifocals and the lightning rod.
4. I represented the United States in France.
5. I was the "First Citizen of Philadelphia," and my picture is on the $100 bill!

Who Am I? _____

Who Am I?

35

1. I am a woman who lived from 1921 to 2006.
2. I was fired from a job because I was pregnant.
3. I am credited with starting the modern womens' liberation movement.
4. I helped found the National Organization for Women (NOW).
5. I wrote the book *The Feminine Mystique*.

 Who Am I? _____

36

1. I am a man who lived from 1805 to 1879.
2. I started my writing career using the pen name Aristides, a Greek name meaning "the Just."
3. I was an abolitionist.
4. I stated that slavery should be ended "immediately."
5. I was the founder of the radical abolitionist paper *The Liberator*.

 Who Am I? _____

37

1. I am a man who lived from 1822 to 1885.
2. I was born in Point Pleasant, Ohio.
3. Abraham Lincoln was one of my best friends.
4. I was the General of the Union Army during the Civil War.
5. I served two terms as president of the United States.

Who Am I? _____

38

1. I am a man who lived from 1757 to 1804.
2. I was born in the British West Indies.
3. I helped found the first national bank.
4. I was one of the writers of the Federalist Papers.
5. I was killed in a duel by Aaron Burr.

Who Am I? _____

39

1. I am a man who lived from 1899 to 1961.
2. I won both a Nobel Prize and a Pulitzer Prize.
3. I was an ambulance driver in Italy in World War I.
4. I was a member of the "Lost Generation."
5. I wrote *A Farewell to Arms* and *The Sun Also Rises*.

 Who Am I? _____

40

1. I am a man who lived from 1874 to 1964.
2. I worked as a mining engineer before getting involved in politics.
3. I defeated Alfred E. Smith in an election.
4. I was president when the Great Depression started.
5. Shantytowns called "Hoovervilles" were named after me!

 Who Am I? _____

41

❶ I am a man who lived from 1767 to 1845.

❷ I grew up on the frontier.

❸ I fought in the War of 1812.

❹ I led U.S. forces against Native Americans in Florida.

❺ I was the seventh president of the United States.

Who Am I? _____

42

❶ I am a man who lived from 1743 to 1826.

❷ I founded the University of Virginia.

❸ My home was Monticello.

❹ I stated that the First Amendment built "a wall of separation between church and state."

❺ I wrote the Declaration of Independence.

Who Am I? _____

43

① I am a man who lived from 1747 to 1792.

② I was born in Scotland.

③ I served on English ships for several years, but then emigrated to the United States.

④ In the Revolutionary War, I became the United States' first well-known naval fighter.

⑤ When asked to surrender, I replied, "I have not yet begun to fight!"

 Who Am I? _____

44

① I am a woman who lived from 1880 to 1968.

② I was born in Alabama.

③ Due to a sickness when I was 19 months old, I became deaf and blind.

④ My teacher was Anne Sullivan.

⑤ I was the first deaf and blind person to earn a Bachelor of Arts degree.

 Who Am I? _____

Who Am I?

45

1. I am a woman who lived from 1859 to 1932.
2. My father was a Congressman.
3. I was a social reformer.
4. I was the general secretary of the National Consumers League.
5. I campaigned against sweatshops, and for child labor laws, minimum wage, and women's suffrage.

 Who Am I? _____

46

1. I am a man who lived from 1917 to 1963.
2. I was born in Massachusetts.
3. I was the youngest president ever elected.
4. I said, "ask not what your country can do for you; ask what you can do for your country."
5. I was assassinated in Dallas in 1963.

 Who Am I? _____

Who Am I?

47

1. I am a man who lived from 1929 to 1968.
2. My father and grandfather were both preachers.
3. I led the Montgomery bus boycott.
4. There is a national holiday named for me.
5. I gave the famous "I Have a Dream" speech in 1963 in Washington, D.C.

Who Am I? _____

48

1. I am a man who lived from 1807 to 1870.
2. I was born on a plantation in Virginia.
3. I graduated from West Point, and later served as its superintendent.
4. I led the Army of Northern Virginia.
5. I surrendered to General Ulysses S. Grant at Appomattox in 1865.

Who Am I? _____

Who Am I?

49

1. I am a man who lived from 1774 to 1809.
2. Natural history was one of my lifelong passions.
3. Thomas Jefferson said I was so honest that whatever I reported "would be as certain as if seen" by Jefferson himself.
4. I served as governor of the Louisiana Territory.
5. I was hired by Jefferson to explore the Louisiana Purchase.

 Who Am I? _____

50

1. I am a man who lived from 1885 to 1951.
2. I grew up in a small town in Minnesota.
3. I was the first American to be awarded the Nobel Prize in literature.
4. I wrote the book *Main Street*.
5. I also wrote *Babbitt*.

 Who Am I? _____

Who Am I?

51

1. I am a man who lived from 1809 to 1865.
2. I am from Illinois.
3. I was at Gettysburg, Pennsylvania.
4. I issued the Emancipation Proclamation.
5. I was the 16th president, and my head is on the penny!

 Who Am I? _____

52

1. I am a man who lived from 1902 to 1974.
2. I was a celebrity in the 1920s.
3. I was a U.S. Air Mail pilot.
4. I flew a plane called the *Spirit of St. Louis*.
5. I was the first person to fly a plane alone across the Atlantic Ocean!

 Who Am I? _____

Who Am I?

53

1. I am a man who lived from 1789 to 1839.
2. I was born in Sussex County, New Jersey.
3. I owned a printing press.
4. I was a Quaker.
5. I was an abolitionist who organized the Abolitionist Union Humane Society in Ohio.

Who Am I? _____

54

1. I am a man who lived from 1751 to 1836.
2. I supported freedom of religion.
3. I wrote some of the Federalist Papers.
4. I am known as the "Father of the Constitution."
5. I was the fourth President of the United States.

Who Am I? _____

55

1. I am a man who lived from 1796 to 1859.
2. My brother-in-law was the famous author Nathaniel Hawthorne.
3. I represented Massachusetts in both the Senate and the House.
4. I was an education reformer.
5. I am called the "Father of American Public Schools."

Who Am I? _____

56

1. I am a man who lived from 1755 to 1835.
2. I served in the Continental Army during the Revolutionary War.
3. I wrote a famous biography of George Washington.
4. I was the Chief Justice of the Supreme Court for 34 years!
5. I established the power of judicial review.

Who Am I? _____

Who Am I?

57

1. I am a man who lived from 1908 to 1993.
2. At school I was forced to write and rewrite the Constitution as punishment; this sparked my interest in the law.
3. I was an attorney in the famous case *Brown* v. *Board of Education*, which ended segregation in schools.
4. Lyndon B. Johnson appointed me to the Supreme Court.
5. I was the first African American to serve on the Supreme Court.

Who Am I? _____

58

1. I am a man who lived from 1809 to 1884.
2. I grew up on a farm in Virginia.
3. I was an inventor.
4. I am known as the "Father of Modern Agriculture."
5. My father tried for 28 years to make a reaper (a machine to harvest grain)—where he failed, I succeeded!

Who Am I? _____

59

❶ I am a man who lived from 1758 to 1831.

❷ I fought in the Revolutionary War.

❸ I was a leader during the "Era of Good Feelings," a time when there was little conflict in politics.

❹ An important foreign policy doctrine is named for me.

❺ I was the fifth president of the United States.

 Who Am I? _____

60

❶ I am a man who lived from 1837 to 1913.

❷ I was a banker and financier.

❸ By 1901 I was one of the wealthiest men in the world.

❹ I used my fortune to stave off a financial crisis.

❺ I am usually known by my initials!

 Who Am I? _____

Who Am I?

61

1. I am a man who lived from 1791 to 1872.
2. My father was a Calvinist pastor.
3. I was a successful portrait painter.
4. There's a certain code named after me.
5. I invented the telegraph.

Who Am I? _____

62

1. I am a woman who lived from 1860 to 1926.
2. My parents were Quakers.
3. I was only five feet tall.
4. I was a sharpshooter.
5. I was one of the star attractions in Buffalo Bill's Wild West Show.

Who Am I? _____

63

❶ I am a man who was born in 1961.

❷ I was born in Hawaii.

❸ I am a prominent member of the Democratic Party.

❹ I represented Illinois as a Senator.

❺ I am the first African American President of the United States.

Who Am I? _____

64

❶ I am a woman who was born in 1930.

❷ I graduated from Stanford Law School.

❸ I served as a judge in Arizona.

❹ President Ronald Reagan appointed me to the Supreme Court in 1983.

❺ I was the first woman to serve on the Supreme Court.

Who Am I? _____

65

1. I am a man who lived from 1737 to 1809.
2. My father was a Quaker.
3. I was a passionate supporter of American independence.
4. I wrote, "These are the times that try men's souls."
5. I wrote the famous pamphlet *Common Sense*.

Who Am I? _____

66

1. I am a woman who lived from 1913 to 2005.
2. I lived in Montgomery, Alabama.
3. I was a seamstress.
4. I worked with Dr. Martin Luther King, Jr.
5. In 1955 I refused to give up my bus seat!

Who Am I? _____

67

1. I am a woman who lived from 1880 to 1965.
2. I graduated from both Mount Holyoke and Columbia University.
3. I was a social activist who supported welfare, benefits, and pensions.
4. I served as Secretary of Labor.
5. I was the first woman appointed to the U.S. Cabinet.

 _____

68

1. I am a man who lived form 1911 to 2004.
2. I was a very successful Hollywood actor.
3. I was the Governor of California for eight years.
4. I was a Republican.
5. I was president during the 1980s.

 _____

Who Am I?

69

1. I am a woman who was born in 1951.
2. I am a nationally ranked tennis player.
3. I am also a physicist.
4. I flew in the Space Shuttle.
5. I was the first female American astronaut.

 Who Am I? _____

70

1. I am a man who lived from 1919 to 1972.
2. I was born into a family of poor sharecroppers.
3. I'm in the Baseball Hall of Fame.
4. I played baseball for the Negro American League in the 1940s.
5. I was the first African American Major League Baseball player.

 Who Am I? _____

Who Am I?

71

1. I am a man who lived from 1839 to 1937.
2. My father was a traveling salesman.
3. I was the first American to make a billion dollars.
4. Today, my name is synonymous with wealth.
5. I founded the Standard Oil Company.

 _____

72

1. I am a woman who lived from 1884 to 1962.
2. I always thought that I was an ugly duckling.
3. I gave many speeches and wrote many articles promoting women's rights.
4. I helped write the United Nations' Universal Declaration of Human Rights.
5. I was a very active First Lady.

 _____

73

1. I am a man who lived from 1882 to 1945.
2. I served as Governor of New York.
3. Polio paralyzed me from the waist down.
4. I put forth the New Deal, a program to provide relief during the Great Depression.
5. I served four terms as president of the United States.

Who Am I? _____

74

1. I am a woman who lived from 1787(?) to 1812.
2. My tribe was the Agaidika, or Salmon Eater, tribe of the Shoshone.
3. A river, a lake, and several mountains in the West are named for me.
4. I accompanied American explorers on a long journey.
5. A dollar coin has my face on it.

Who Am I? _____

Who Am I?

75

1. I am a man who lived from 1795 to 1858.
2. I was born into slavery in Virginia.
3. I lived in both a slave state and a free state.
4. I sued for my freedom.
5. The landmark Supreme Court decision that carries my name declared slaves to be property.

Who Am I? _____

76

1. I am a man who lived from 1878 to 1968.
2. I entered college at age 13.
3. I won the Pulitzer Prize for journalism.
4. I was a "muckraker."
5. I wrote *The Jungle*, a book that exposed poor sanitation and working conditions in meat-packing factories.

Who Am I? _____

77

1. I am a man who lived from 1831(?) to 1890.
2. I was born in what is now South Dakota.
3. I was a leader of the Hunkpapa Band of the Teton Sioux.
4. I was a medicine man who encouraged resistance to white invasion.
5. I inspired the fighters who defeated Lieutenant Colonel George A. Custer in the Battle of Little Bighorn.

 _____

78

1. I am a man who lived from 1580 to 1631.
2. I was born in England but sailed to America.
3. I made some of the first maps of Virginia and New England.
4. I was captured by the Powhatan Indians and rescued by a young Indian girl.
5. I led the settlers of Jamestown, Virginia.

 _____

79

❶ I am a man who lived from 1585(?) to 1622.

❷ I was from the Patuxet tribe.

❸ I learned English after being kidnapped by English fishermen and taken to Spain and then England.

❹ When I escaped back to America, I learned that most of my tribe had been killed by European diseases.

❺ I helped the Pilgrims survive the first winter in the New World.

 _____

80

❶ I am a woman who lived from 1815 to 1902.

❷ I lived in Seneca Falls, New York.

❸ I wanted women to be able to vote and have other rights.

❹ With Susan B. Anthony, I founded the National Women Suffrage Association.

❺ With Lucretia Mott, I held the first women's rights convention.

 _____

81

1. I am a woman who lived from 1811 to 1896.
2. My father was a Presbyterian minister.
3. I was part of the Underground Railroad, which helped runaway slaves escape to the North.
4. My brother was the clergyman Henry Ward Beecher and my sister was the educator Catherine Beecher.
5. I wrote *Uncle Tom's Cabin*.

Who Am I? _____

82

1. I am a man who lived from 1840 to 1910.
2. I taught at Yale University.
3. I was the first person in the United States to teach a course called "sociology."
4. I created the term "ethnocentrism."
5. I wrote a book called *Folkways*.

Who Am I? _____

83

1. I am a man who lived from 1857 to 1930.
2. I was born in Cincinnati, Ohio.
3. I was the first Governor-General of the Philippines.
4. I stood 6 feet 2 inches tall and I weighed more than 300 pounds!
5. I was the 27th president of the United States—and later the Chief Justice on the Supreme Court.

Who Am I? _____

84

1. I am a woman who lived from 1857 to 1944.
2. My father was in the oil business.
3. I was one of the first investigative journalists.
4. I was a "muckraker."
5. My book, *History of the Standard Oil Company*, exposed the company's unfair ways of doing business.

Who Am I? _____

85

1. I am a man who lived from 1784 to 1850.
2. I was a poor student, and I was embarrassed about my writing all my life.
3. I spent 40 years in the U.S. military, and fought in three wars.
4. I became a national hero during the Mexican War.
5. I was the 12th President of the United States.

Who Am I? _____

86

1. I am a man who lived from 1817 to 1862.
2. I was a lifelong abolitionist.
3. Ralph Waldo Emerson was a friend and mentor of mine.
4. I wrote *Walden,* a book praising simple living in natural surroundings.
5. I also wrote the essay "Civil Disobedience."

Who Am I? _____

87

1. I am a man who lived from 1893 to 1953.
2. I was a celebrity in the 1920s.
3. I wrote a book called *Match Play and the Spin of the Ball*.
4. I was the first American to win the Wimbledon Championship in England.
5. My nickname was "Big Bill."

Who Am I? _____

88

1. I am a man who lived from 1884 to 1972.
2. I grew up in Independence, Missouri.
3. I fought in World War I.
4. I made the phrase "the buck stops here" popular.
5. I authorized the use of atomic bombs on Japan.

Who Am I? _____

89

1. I am a man who lived from 1861 to 1932.
2. I was a historian.
3. I thought that the American character was formed by American expansion.
4. I was mostly interested in the effect of the frontier.
5. My most famous essay is "The Significance of the Frontier in American History."

Who Am I? _____

90

1. I am a man who lived from 1835 to 1910.
2. I grew up in Missouri alongside the Mississippi River.
3. As a boy, I wanted to be a riverboat pilot.
4. My real name was Samuel Clemens.
5. I wrote *The Adventures of Tom Sawyer* and *Adventures of Huckleberry Finn*.

Who Am I? _____

91

1. I am a man who lived from 1794 to 1877.
2. I started working on ferries and steamboats when I was 11.
3. My nickname was "the Commodore."
4. I made fortune in steamships and, later, railroads.
5. There is a university in Nashville named for me.

 _____

92

1. I am a man who lived from 1451(?) to 1512.
2. I worked for Lorenzo de' Medici, the same person Leonardo DaVinci worked for.
3. I was an explorer.
4. My writings about South America were widely read in Europe.
5. A variation of my name was used to name two continents!

 _____

93

1. I am a man who lived from 1856 to 1915.
2. I was born into slavery.
3. I served as an advisor to two presidents.
4. I was willing to accept segregation in exchange for economic development.
5. I was the founder and first leader of the all-black Tuskegee Institute.

Who Am I? _____

94

1. I am a man who lived from 1732 to 1799.
2. When I was young, I worked as a surveyor.
3. I led troops in the Revolutionary War.
4. My home was Mount Vernon.
5. I was the first president of the United States!

Who Am I? _____

❶ I am a man who lived from 1819 to 1892.

❷ I thought all religions were equal.

❸ I celebrated the vitality of American democracy.

❹ I wrote of life and death in "Out of the Cradle Endlessly Rocking."

❺ I published a book of poetry titled *Leaves of Grass*.

 _____

❶ I am a man who lived from 1765 to 1825.

❷ I was born in Massachusetts to farmers.

❸ I manufactured muskets.

❹ I came up with the idea of interchangeable parts in machines.

❺ I invented the cotton gin.

 _____

Who Am I?

97

1. I am a man who lived from 1856 to 1924.
2. I served as president of Princeton University.
3. I put forth "Fourteen Points."
4. I was an advocate of the League of Nations.
5. I was president of the United States during World War I.

Who Am I? _____

98

1. I am a man who lived from 1871 to 1948.
2. I lived in Ohio.
3. I worked as a bicycle mechanic.
4. My brother's name was Wilbur.
5. I was the first person to fly an airplane!

Who Am I? _____

99

1. I am a man who lived from 1867 to 1912.
2. I lived in Ohio.
3. My favorite childhood toy was a paper-and-bamboo "helicopter."
4. My brother's name was Orville.
5. I was the second person to fly an airplane!

Who Am I? _____

100

1. I am a man who lived from 1801 to 1877.
2. I led a great march from Illinois to Utah.
3. I served as governor of the Territory of Utah.
4. I succeeded Joseph Smith.
5. I was the second president of the Church of Latter-Day Saints.

Who Am I? _____

www.ingramcontent.com/pod-product-compliance
Lightning Source LLC
LaVergne TN
LVHW061343060426
835512LV00016B/2651